Poems

James
Knox Whittet

Foreword
Pauline Stainer

To Douglas

With best wishes

From James Knox Whittet

November, 2012

First published 2012 by IRON Press
5 Marden Terrace
Cullercoats
North Shields
NE30 4PD
tel/fax +44(0)191 2531901
ironpress@blueyonder.co.uk
www.ironpress.co.uk

FIRST EDITION

ISBN 978-0-9565725-2-3
Printed by Field Print, Boldon Colliery

© James Knox Whittet 2012

Typeset in 11pt Georgia
Cover artwork by Mandy Tait
Book design and lay-out by
Peter Mortimer, Brian Grogan & Kate Jones

IRON Press Books are distributed by Central Books
and represented by Inpress Ltd, Churchill House,
12 Mosley Street, Newcastle upon Tyne, NE1 1DE
Tel: 44(0) 191 230 8104
www.inpressbooks.co.uk

THE POEMS

BIOGRAPHY

JAMES KNOX WHITTET was born and brought up in the Hebridean Island of Islay where his father was head gardener at Dunlossit Castle. His paternal grandmother came from a crofting family on the Isle of Skye. James was educated at Keills Primary in Islay, Newbattle Abbey College and Cambridge University. His pamphlet, *A Brief History Of Devotion* (The Hawthorn Press) was published in 2003. In 2004, his pamphlet, *Seven Poems for Engraved Fishermen* (Meniscus Press) was shortlisted for the Callum MacDonald Award from the National Library of Scotland.

In the same year, he received an award from the Society of Authors. He edited the anthology *100 Island Poems* (IRON Press), published in 2005 which was nominated by *The Scotsman* as one of the Books of the Year and received a major award from the Arts Council of England. He also edited the companion volume, *Writers On Islands* (IRON Press), published in 2008. James won the George Crabbe Memorial Award in 2004, 2005, 2008 and 2011. In 2009, he won the Neil Gunn Memorial Award for poetry and an award from Highland Arts. In 2010 his translation of Sorley MacLean's *Hallaig* was commended in *The Times* Stephen Spender Prize. The spoken word CD of his poems entitled *Dark Islands* was released in 2011. This is his first full poetry collection.

To Ann

FOREWORD

THIS IS A QUIETLY AMAZING collection of poetry. It moves full circle from Kafka's meeting with Einstein to a final poem about Einstein in Cromer. Its eclectic range includes Wittgenstein as a presiding spirit in Connemara, Dante in Auschwitz and Virginia Woolf on Skye. There are memories of an island childhood, landscapes, seascapes, lost traditions. The poems unfold with great patience in a variety of verse form and breadth of line. Everything, unusually, is given time.

James Knox Whittet's Islay background may account for this. Anyone who has heard him read his poems, will have been struck by their incantatory quality. Each island is its own kingdom, shot through with skerry and lighthouse, the rustle of light on water. Fields are still scythed, oats stand in stooks. Crofters' ghosts rise from the lazybeds. The lives and deaths of St. Kilda are probed with great subtlety by the poet. For the dead still listen and wait.

The observation in these poems is sharply sensuous. The dipping of 'varnished oars into peated water', 'green and silver bands of mackerel', the 'burnt honey scent of gorse'. An island childhood is suffused with salt and peat smoke, the furling and unfurling of descended swans, the way anchored lilies whiten a loch. Particularly brilliant is the treatment of light, its behaviour between remote isles, the exchange between lucidity and reflection. Detail is meticulous in all the poems. Kafka's father is caught slumped asleep, his forehead imprinted with 'washable ink' from the unread newspaper.

The vitality of poetry stems partly from wonderful oppositions. James Knox Whittet's sestina for *Wittgenstein in Connemara* and his poem *Virginia Woolf on Skye* are examples of such crossings. They allow the writer release from his island background, and spring from the tension between outgoing and holding back. The poet can throw glimmering tangents, as well as evoke 'daylight's undersides'. These glimpses, at a remove so to speak, give the writer freedom from his awareness of being alone in the crowd.

In these many-layered poems, one complexity hatches another. A retarded child's experience of abuse by a priest is suggested obliquely through borrowed words. In the magnificent *Peaches*, memory momentarily transfigures a hospice. Fruit are plucked again by the dying with infinite tenderness. Each peach folded in tissue with its downy cleavage, boxed and left on chilled marble in the castle pantry. All this caught delicately under the merciful bewilderment of diamorphine.

James Knox Whittet writes with deep compassion. Those slow and biblical 'silences of God' which were part of an islander's way of being, sustain his writing. Etty Hillesum still walks with her lost children in the luminously unfenced fields of peppery lupins.

Pauline Stainer

WHEN KAFKA MET EINSTEIN

WHEN KAFKA MET EINSTEIN

You listened with your wolf-like ears,
in background, as always, while he
harangued his devotees with bewildering
concepts of space and time and motion.

You were no stranger to bewilderment:
alone at night in your room, gazing down
on the ant-like citizens of Prague who
scurried along labyrinthine corridors of

streets, with the mythical figure of your
father ensconced below you in a deep armchair,
like a throne: asleep, his forehead imprinted
with washable ink from the unread newspaper.

In the womb of this room, you gestated
the alien bodies of your lovers: Felice, Julie, Milena . . .
exploring them and yourself in indelible letter
after letter, bridging chasms with the mathematical

constructs of your imperturbable sentences.
Here too, you dreamed of Gregor Samsa:
a man of obsessive, mechanical habits who,
like yourself, spent his leisure hours on

imaginary journeys through railway timetables,
and who awoke to find that his body had
rebelled against him in the dark, leaving him
shamefully unable to catch his regular train to work.

Like Einstein, you transformed our conception
of the world by dreaming of the motions
of trains which accelerated to the speed of
light and you waved your bloodied handkerchief

to rows of absolutes left standing on the platform.

Between 1910 and 1912, Franz Kafka frequently met Albert Einstein at a
salon in Prague. Einstein's study of train schedules and train motion had a
profound influence on the development of the theory of relativity.

TRANSMUTABILITY

Last night I dreamed about you ... all I know is that we kept merging into
each other ... but here too the uncertainty of transmutability entered.
– Kafka in a letter to Milena.

In the cut-glass of evening with the animal city
kept at bay behind panes and smothering curtains,
I caress the insubstantial dream of your body with my pen.
Father, my judge and silent confessor, sits monumentally
in the room below me as I magnify myself with
ink at this heavy desk: supported on his shoulders.
Each letter I form is a needle which penetrates my
flesh like the tooth of a harrow until recognition
incinerates my eyes when each sentence is complete.
I wound myself so that you might enter and our
insect limbs become so entangled that I no longer
know where you end and I begin as I journey through
corridors which lead nowhere and everywhere to stand,
at last, in front of one who will inform me of my crime.

A BRIEF HISTORY OF DEVOTION

For then we should know the mind of God.
– Stephen Hawking

They pack auditoriums to hear you,
worshippers of the loose-limbed oracle
whose electric voice reverberates
through those vast interstices where God hides.
Out of the black hole of the stage's wing,
you glide silently and effortlessly
on oiled wheels: a warrior bruised by stars;
your screened dictionary of revealed truths
mounted on technology's chariot:
wisdom's dark matter spread and lit before you.

Pilgrims applaud beneath your lifted feet,
brushed by particles of light reflected
from your highlighted singularity,
touched by radiation that bears your name.
The dreamlike, disembodied voice resounds
through silence, stripped of all those accidents
of man; intimate as any machine:
impersonality that breaks the heart.

Your expressive eyebrows ascend and fall
as you slyly wink at the Creator
whose cunning mind you expect soon to know.
You intersperse your universal sermon
with witticisms, anxious to reveal
that, like Him, you're no stranger to a joke:
authors both of little read bestsellers,
questions with answers no one can translate;
immune to time but not to suffering,
lost among those interstellar spaces.

Like disintegrating comets, your eyes
burn, fixed beneath footlights that soon will fade
into that curved past where the future resides,
leaving your transatlantic voice behind:
that advertiser's dream that will live on
without the body it never possessed,
persuading us to go on conversing,
whatever the cost, as those radio
telescopes lengthen into the night sky
to catch echoes of voices: not our own.

IN MEMORY OF R.S. THOMAS

I see you with your sparse locks of
greying hair lifted by sea winds as you
stand gazing skywards, your eyes following
the guided flight paths of sea birds.

Your past, a litany of place names:
Anglesey, Eglwys-fach, Manafon,
Aberdaron around which the haunting
images fold like burning birch leaves.

You knelt at the altars of stubborn,
stone churches on that borderland of doubt
and belief, your ears attuned to those moorland
silences in which that bewildering God resides.

Sometimes the plain words of your prayers
would ignite and an arrow of sunlight would
pierce the stained glass and painted figures
would move as if in an eternal dance

like the atoms in physicists' strange tables
in which solidity exists only in our minds.
Your footsteps echo no longer down those still
lanes of Lynn, scented with the desiccated coconut

of gorse and misted with the vapours of
cattle's breath rising from behind high hedges.
In remote cottages, the old would spin yarns of
loneliness in the slow treadmills of dreams.

Do you continue with your fierce questioning
now you've merged with your loved Welsh loam?
Or are your powdered ears tuned only to the sea's
slow intakes of breath on nights pillared with frost

when willow wands of smelted moonlight cradle
Ynys Enlli which lies just out of reach, as
always, across the Sound where the ghosts of dead
saints step through green seas of lush grass?

Your ashes lie just outwith the church you
could never wholly enter as you explored that
adult geometry of the mind where acute angles
dissected angles like your wife's intricate veins.

God's rebellious angel, you placed words like
stepping stones to bridge the gaps between
islands of meaning which float in vast oceans
over which a watered rainbow sometimes arcs.

CUTTINGS

*A sort of cutting taken from one person and grafted on to the heart of
another continues to carry on its existence even when the person from
whom it had been detached has died.*
– Marcel Proust.

In the visible breath of early spring,
you'd sieve leaf mould
onto the potting shed bench:
sifting darkness and sunbeams

beneath the cracked skylight
where sycamores swayed
broken shadows of their limbs
in risen sea winds.

On the paraffin stove,
a pan of loam would steam
to sterilization: all impurities
transmuted into clouds

to darken the rafters and hang
globes of moisture in the embroidery
of the spider's loom.
Across the stone floor,

you'd leave records of your steps
in the crushed orange
of clay pots, making intricate
markings that would remain.

In the white dust of hormone
rooting powder, you'd dip the angled
cuttings of carnations and ring
each filled pot with grey leafed stems,

lowered into fingered hollows.
In tiny polythene tents, they'd sweat
until translucent tendrils of root took
hold as you took hold of my hand

in that tented ward where all footprints
were swabbed before they settled:
all traces of grief removed;
above you, panelled roof panes sealed.

Days later, I helped lower you
into frosted loam that steamed in
misted sunlight: the dressed cord leaving
angled markings on my soiled fingers.

IMPRINTS

In your left bag, your cotton gloves remain,
with those few copper coins, grown green with age;
the folded that that kept your perm from rain;
the envelope that held Dad's final wage;
the twisted tube of mints you saved for church;
the oval mirror that won't show your face;
that linen hanky you will no more touch:
all those loved things are kept and stored in place.

Free from dust motes that waltz through summer haze,
they sit in state behind those cupboard doors
in that front room you kept for special days
where elms slide shadows across polished floors.

Those fading imprints only I can find:
you have become all that you have left behind.

ECHOES

A lady still, she sits in state among cats;
portraits of ancestors, imperious on walls,
politely ignoring the droppings of bats:
more accustomed to gaze from marbled halls.

Out of the top drawer, she dines on her own,
a tray brought to her with sausage, egg and chips;
an armchair displaying its coiled springs: her throne,
cursing her servant for letting standards slip.

Outside, where mists ascend the fields of autumn,
geese loudly patrol in pairs the unhinged gates:
warning strangers, guarding treasures that have gone;
in the porch, a roped, rusted bell hangs and waits

for those aristocrats who no longer come.
Elgar's cello laments as the record plays,
dust creating a vibrato of its own,
heightening the poignancy of remembered days:

gardeners pacing soundlessly over lawns;
islanded beds where jeweled roses swayed
in late summer breezes moistened by oceans;
the striped croquet lawn where white-clad figures played,

their moving shadows crossed by flight paths of quail.
Those Edwardian times: the poor in their place
until choked by gas in trenches in those pale
Flanders' dawns: terror burned into each young face.

That estate subsided with the mines that failed
where miners bowed their heads in deference to beams
and stunted ponies heaved trolleys along railed
darkness to where the low coal face dripped and gleamed

in the ghostly light from lamps. Her father's heart
stopped along with the swift flow of coal and cash;
her husband drank; the house with its hard earned art
was sold, trees felled: flames of autumn turned to ash.

Widowed, worn with the slow reductions of years,
she lives in the lodge by the arthritic gates,
maintaining the divisions whose loss she fears,
her reflection drowned by grease on silver plates.

Some nights, when fire breathes as it consumes coal
and flames' long shadows shiver in sudden draughts,
each spent hour signalled by the antique clock's toll:
owls call like cries echoing from closed mine shafts.

LAWRENCE OF ARABIA IN COLLIESTON

Here where the very earth vibrates with the thunder
of wave after wave against black, slabbed rocks, you
take shelter from the storms of the world in this
hovel balanced on heron's legs above the North Sea.

You watch shadows of coal flames scrawl indecipherable
words across stoned walls as you sit and suck pandrops
to soothe the ache of remembrance. Somewhere above you,
searching, swooping gulls cry out their echoing loneliness.

In haared afternoons, you stride the consuming dunes of Forvie:
that desert of the north, with its oases of blackened heather
where camouflaged grouse cower and explode into ragged flight,
rabbits sound silenced alarms with the blizzards of their tails.

Each night, you hear the sea at your feet lick its old sores as
you lie buried in blankets, out of reach of past blinding suns.

*In 1930, T.E. Lawrence, who came to despise the publicity which
surrounded his exploits as Lawrence of Arabia, lived in a primitive
cottage in the remote fishing village of Collieston on the north-east
coast of Scotland.*

MOVING WITH THE TIMES

He sat in the back row of the classroom
drawing the faces of clocks, his blunted
pencil rounding a smudged penny, the drum
of rain sounding on the corrugated
roof, dates eroding at his fingertips.
In each separate circle, both short hands
would reach unsteadily to numbers scrawled
around the frayed circumference, his lips
pursed; engrossed in motions of time while strands
of weak sunlight, when the rain had ceased, sprawled

across distempered walls where maps, stained pink,
were stretched out between two pins. He was born
with a fault, his brain unable to link
his thoughts: a jigsaw with the pieces too worn
to fit. He worked on the croft, his mother,
widowed, took in men to stretch her income.
When moving woodwormed floorboards had settled
down for the night and the moon formed rivers
of light across faded linoleum
flowers, he'd listen as trapped sheep wrestled

with fences making tightened, barbed wires strum.
Mornings, in his black wellies, overturned
and greying, he'd shove barrowloads of dung
beneath wet, arched trees; on the loch, swans preened
their dark brood; above his bent head, white-fronted
geese arrowed for the ocean and left pale
reflections of themselves on stilled water.
A tractor brought mounds of clay into bleached
lines in fields where worms were upturned to veils
of gulls. In misted light, buzzards loitered

in moist gulfs of air. He died an old man
of twenty-seven, leaving behind heaps
of nameless jotters, their pages of worn
circles moving with the times. Those keepsakes
his mother burnt in a tidying fit
with ripped empty, yellow bags of hen feed:
dog-eared pages curled in flames extended
by stray breezes making flecks of ash flit
and rise and drawn, unsteady hands recede
as singed circumferences contracted.

THE LAST MAN ON JURA

"We shall meet in the place where there is no darkness."

On those lucid Hebridean evenings
of summer when the branched antlers of stags
are mirrored on shifting lochans, weaving
reflections like drowning fingers; greylags
shadowing the sea's light, you gather driftwood
left stranded by tides, your arms raised,
annihilating those thoughts that gnaw your mind
down the long, stone corridors written with blood
to that numbered room where fear lurks to erase
undesirable meanings of the last man.

The Paps of Jura follow your every move
as peewits empty their bowls of liquid music
to fill the silence that stalks from the moor.
You return to Barnhill where the wick
of the single candle moves in its lighted dance
of the *ancient time* reviving ghosts
of the abolished past scented with fallen
bluebells before the mind's disciplined trance
by priests of fact who dam history's flow
until all that is real is a shared dream.

Afternoons, you lift brown trout from chocolate lochs,
whitened by anchored lilies; in the bay,
ringed with sounding whins, you lie back,
resting on nothingness, facing the sky
to count the constant number of held clouds
beyond the penal colonies of fiction
where words are trapped like ravenous rats in cages
and life laid flat in shelved, dusted records:
you drift on the slow waves' deviations
to some still untouched place where darkness is.

George Orwell wrote most of 'Nineteen Eighty Four', originally entitled
'The Last Man In Europe', on the Hebridean island of Jura. Words in
italics from 'Nineteen Eighty Four'.

THE COMMA BUTTERFLY

On the walls of a Nazi holding cell,
children, waiting in terror their turn
for the *showers*, scrawled butterfly after
butterfly in heavenly flight from stone.

On the underside of each blooded,
ragged wing, each comma,
each pause for breath, appeared
to be in the form of a question mark.

PEACHES

Peaches ... peaches: yet again you mutter
as the wind shifts folds of mauve curtains
along the half-open French window, shuttered
against sunlight, bringing with it those scents
of cow dung from that farm across fenced fields
of neeps that raise their pale, undersided
leaves in rows merging in waves of light.
Below the leaf-strew lawn, a stripped hedge shields
the hospice from the trunk road on which tides
of lighted traffic flood the lengthened night.

The diamorphine, with mechanical
insistence, hisses into your bruised veins,
distancing you from pain with clinical
efficiency as the life you lived drains
slowly out of reach, leaving you to gaze
down on yourself like some lone wood pigeon
peering down from the high garden wall as
dawn exposed the brassicas in those rays
of light sieved through mist when sweet peas burgeon
on trellises hung with spiders' moist gauze.

Oblongs of tinfoil, silver, red and gold
were stretched across strands of green, oily twine;
they glinted as they were shaken by cold
sea breezes that traced your dry lips with brine
when you rose at dawn each day in summer,
pulling on your trousers stained by the punnet
of red gooseberries you sat on when you slipped,
but you'd arrive to find those gossamers
on jewelled sprouts broken, leaves serrated
and the frail, swollen branches of veins ripped.

Peaches ... peaches: your strangled, muffled cries
break through again in that room burdened by
the high, cribbed bed you struggle to rise
from in your delirium as you try
to escape from the present moment
to the life that was: I see you transfer
the pollen from one pink, pouting flower
to another, rabbit's tail at the point
of a cane; paraffin fumes would linger
and floating flecks of snowcem would shower

the air scented with geranium leaves;
stained panes of shadowed glass held together
with still soft putty veined beneath the eaves
where birds in their unseen cage would gather
their last breaths to break free. In the morning,
you stood and sprayed peated water along
the shoots trained with raffia on looped wire,
your thumb on the end of coiled hose making
rainbows arch and globules of water hang
as if suspended in the sunlit air.

Days before they were due for the *Big House*,
you would ease the downed fruit from its slender
stem with fingers curved around its cleavage
and fold each one in tissues with tender
care. Those peaches were left to blush alone
in that locked shed where breaths of summer air
penetrated the mossed, loosened windows
and orange dust from crushed clay pots was blown
across the shaft of light along the door
and rising winds at night would form frescoes

of dust on walls. You could never settle
until you delivered those boxed peaches
and left them on the chilled, marble table
in the castle pantry where light reaches
through meshed windows and spreads itself
in pieces across the grained, slabbed, stone floor.
You paused as if to listen to the measures
of the loud, brass clock on the high, slim shelf;
reluctantly, you turned towards the door:
no place was safe enough for such treasures.

And now, they come at you again: drugged
to death. They loom up from linoleum
shining with disinfectant and flooded
with fractured moon faces of your family.
Above your head, hangs a globe suspended
by the slender stem of its flex, folding
soft, orange rays around your withered face
and you reach towards that light, fingers curved
on your right hand, wrist turning on nothing;
eyes staring: still searching for some safe place.

DANTE IN AUSCHWITZ
(For Primo Levi)

I see you standing in Auschwitz still
struggling to recall those lines of Dante
as if your life depended on the lucidity
of language in a world in which words

had been degraded and turned to ash.
Like Communion bread and wine, you shared
those precious fragments that flooded your
mind with your companion in Hell.

Those few words, more precious than soup,
had to be shared to make them real:
You were made men,
to follow after knowledge and excellence.

As a sudden scent of laburnum in May
when a breeze lifts the hanging racemes
and showers of perfumed petals form tides
across the dewed lawn, those words bring home

something deeply known and yet forgotten.
You climbed out of the pit, hand over fist,
on the delicate tendrils of Terza Rima,
bringing another with you on the shoulders

of memory. You became a witness, not a mere
victim, stripped of name and culture and humanity.
You heard those words as if for the first time
like the blast of a trumpet or the voice of God

or like Etty Hillesum, gazing over fields of yellow lupins
burnished by the golden rays of July sunlight
with the evenings transfigured by the moon
casting molten silver across strands of barbed wire,

sensing that suffering and beauty are deeply
intertwined as twins rocked by invisible hands
in the one cradle: back and forth, back and forth
or cotton grass moved by winds on the moor.

In the act of translation, you found that pure
language that lies beneath the Babel of tongues you heard
from men layered each night, like the whispering dead,
on tiers, their nostrils burnt raw by human smoke.

Only a phrase eluded you, a few connecting words
which might bridge the chasm between life
and truth and make all clear: some lucid loch
where a swan forms an arch with its own reflection.

FIRES OF MEMORY

You who once ploughed hedged Norfolk
fields which slope to the sea in blizzards
of gulls, found yourself in Bergen-Belsen
confronting heaps of naked, entangled bodies:

as if clinging to each other in the agony
and loneliness of their separate deaths.
You were sent to liberate but for those,
the freedom that you brought, came too late.

You entered each numbered block, unable
to absorb the horror which was contained
within: tier after tier of the living dead:
their eyes made wild with bottomless pain.

When war, at last, ended, you returned
to that farm where ghosts of winds
open and close pathways through barley
and stilled evenings reverberate with rooks.

But memories of mountains of children's shoes
spilled from each cupboard you opened;
glaciers of eyeless spectacles stared back
at you like sun strands on splintered glass.

You knew you had to give a voice to those
whose voices had been choked by gas.
You gave talks to classrooms of children
and tried to impart the pain behind the facts.

You invited survivors of the Holocaust
to show the tattooed numbers on their arms
and share their nightmares of that time
when they and their loved ones slipped out of time.

School trips to Nazi death camps were arranged
and you watched crocodiles of boys and girls file
past those empty shoes; the watches; gold teeth;
the hair like stubble before the fields are burnt.

I've made it my life's mission to ensure
that people don't forget: you told me,
a week before you died, your voice a harsh
whisper through cancer constricted lungs.

As I stood above your grave, alone in the crowd,
I glanced at gorse which glowed in June sunlight
and I raised my hand as if to catch your torch
to keep the fires of memory burning and burning ...

HANDS

The pathways you opened
have all been closed;
those greenhouses still standing,
but the panes fallen
onto cinders to return
acute angles of light,
at evening.

I circle the garden
on paths of mossed grass,
passing the beds
where memories sleep
until awakened by steps
that have at last
come home.

The soil you turned
has turned back on itself;
that wall, where delphiniums
pencilled moving
measurements of themselves,
stares at me blankly,
in denial.

When I close the door
behind me, plums at dusk
will drop from traceries
of limbs unpruned,
with no sound, as if
into your hands, still cupped
and held.

INFINITE WHEELS

Unmoving, you move through the mountains
of Wicklow still. Eyes closed to the coming
darkness, *the old haunts never more present.*
You propel your imagined wheels in unvarying
circles like the rims of Vico's history where
cycles of sufferings revolve like riddled leaves.

I see you pedal impassively along confined
roads across moors where dark pools reflect
altering sequences of cloud; the angular
spaces between pyramids of peat shot through
with pellets of sunlight as the sea entices
in the smoked distance with its waves.

The tramps in your plays wear invisible
cycle clips long after they've lost their bikes;
they pine for their days of effortless motion:
happily downhill all the way with the scented
wind sifting their sparse locks of hair, beating
back the too solid air in their eternal figures of 8.

Like you, they long for that stillness
of cycling motion: that sensuous sail past
hedged fields where cattle revolve their jaws
on regurgitated grass. I see you again, on your
bed of death, raise your leaded right leg
to mount once more those infinite wheels.

*In his last years, Samuel Beckett, when closing his eyes, was transported
to the loved landscape he cycled through as a child. Bicycles recur
throughout his works. Godot was said to be named after a leading
competitor in the Tour de France. Beckett was influenced by cyclical
historical theories of the seventeenth century Italian philosopher, Vico.
Words in italics taken from Beckett's writings.*

VIRGINIA WOOLF ON SKYE

Eleven years after you wrote
To The Lighthouse, you at last
set foot on Skye and see the unimaginable
contours of the Cuillins stare pitilessly

at themselves in the sea loch's mirrored hall.
Like living in a jellyfish lit up
with green light: you wrote home.
That garden of elms and apple scents

in St. Ives belongs to a different
world of train stations and chintz hotels.
Here on this island where, in stoned places,
only the gable ends of crofts still stand

to angle moonlight and the ghosts of ancestors
scythe still those once gold flecked fields of oats.
But here too, time passes, leaving traces
whose delicate patterns only you can articulate,

and islanders dream, like you, of
some other island where a high,
intermittent light beckons and beckons
from the far side of pain.

CIRCLES OF FIRE

They cannot conceive how it is possible for any mortal to express the
conceptions of his mind in such black characters upon white paper.
– Martin Martin, *A Late Voyage To St. Kilda. (1698)*

You brought the written word
to those islands where voices,
song and memory reigned to keep
the terrors of the dark at bay.

On luminous afternoons, the sundial
of rocks was caressed by time's restless
shadow; gannets exploded into mirrored
surfaces of bays beneath blizzards of cliffs.

On cupped evenings of summer
when Atlantic winds contained their
breath, fulmars floated above themselves
in shards of sunlight on suspended

wings, and the angular green fields
of corn were flecked with gold
between crossed stone walls, veined
with the orange dyes of lichens,

while, on the hill, the forefathers slept
beneath their coarse quilts of heather.
How could all of this be reduced
to scrawled lines on scraps of paper?

In Hirta's parliament where the
measured council of the elders' voices
rose above the Babel of the gulls,
there was no need for *Hansard*,

and in the Gaelic ballads, crooned
around the centered circles of fire
each night, the spoken word travelled
through mysteries of smoke to echo

beyond where ink could reach.

BORROWED WORDS

You learn your lines by heart, leaning across
iron bars of an unhinged gate, watching
raindrops slide down the glistening spines of gorse;
reflections of hills wavering on the surface
of the sea loch; crowded salmon arching
their backs in cages, forming arcs of watered
light when stranded clouds in layers dispersed.
At your feet, midges rise from expanded pools;
a jet engraves the sky, cattle are scattered
over fields hedged in stone. You practice words
like scales, savouring them as your tongue rolls
around lost rhythms only you had heard.

A childhood endured in a Catholic home
for the retarded with its dormitory
of fear; rigid beneath blankets, hearing winds moan
through moors, waiting for that priest's quickened breath,
his harsh, whispered words that stalk your memory
still with meanings your mind could never hold:
flames rising on chapel walls with shadowed stealth
leapt through your brain until it was over; candles
lit for the dying; requests for prayers scrawled
on lined paper pinned to the board; a voice
echoing from the altar; loose-strapped sandals
punishing stone floors; air weighted with incense

in that cathedral on the esplanade
with the Isle of Kerrera safe across the bay;
a yacht dividing molten sea like some blade
of light. When your schooling in shame had ended,
they sent you to this farm where winds comb fields of hay;
frost forms fronds on troughs you can hardly bear to break.
At nights, in a room of your own, voices ascend
from your pocket radio in pained waves

of interference; you listen, wide awake,
to foreigners drowning in crossed stations;
turning words like stones to find one that saves
as if to regain some taken possession.

AISLES

I glimpse her in the aisle of fruit and veg
where black, Israeli grapes sweat in slit bags;
we move closer at the freezer aisle's edge;
bow our heads to inspect the free range eggs.

Beneath strips of light and Muzac of love,
I stalk the path of her reluctant wheels:
hear *Special Offers* announced from above;
avoid the aisle where the shelf-packer kneels.

Sunday after Sunday, on the peals of nine,
I step out in our slow, separate waltz
with a partner unaware she is mine:
advances unspoken can't be repulsed.

No voice or touch to extinguish love's fires:
like God, I mould her to my own desires.

3 A.M. AT NEWPORT PAGNELL SERVICE STATION

I slide my wood effect tray along
the smudged metal runway with iconic
images above my head of frothing cups
of cappuccino, Danish pastries, summits of glistening
baked beans and burnished beef burgers hung
like Vermeers from brightly painted walls.

I carry my frothless coffee to a table
beside the massive panes of the window
through which traffic, grown strangely
silent, forms six strings of a diamond necklace
of red and white lights into the darkness
with no beginning and no end in sight.

Across the aisle, a woman who has strayed
from a Hopper painting, sits alone and keeps searching
through her handbag as if in search of some
official document that might tell her who she
is and why she sits here in this room, laid bare
by fluorescent strips, at 3 a.m. on the 6th of March.

At another table, a man with a beard endlessly
rotates a tea bag in a white mug with a spoon.
I gaze at the slow rotations of the spoon and see
how the colour of his tea deepens and darkens.
An elderly woman with her hair in a bun, bends
her head over a crossword: in search of answers.

I sip my chilling coffee and listen to Sinatra
crooning from the dead. With lowered eyes, I
create patterns from the varying islands of the spilt
blood of tomato ketchup left by former customers
and wonder what decipherable patterns I might leave
behind when I choose to rejoin the necklace of lights below.

I look up again at my few fellow pilgrims
who have entered, like me, by chance into
an unsleeping communion of silence in this glass
cathedral, scented not with incense but with frying oil,
built for travelers who take time out of their journeys
to destinations not wholly of their own choosing.

SEA WINDS

You prayed for a dry morning each Monday.
You would get up early to begin the weekly
wash and I'd see you bent over that deep
stone sink, your bare arms foamed with *Omo*.

In the chilled scullery, the window would stream
with condensation and Jura would dissolve
across the Sound of Islay where the tides
altered their bronchitic breathing with the moon.

The piles of strangled clothing would grow
higher at your side, laid out like throttled
snakes, until you loaded them into the wicker
basket, crowned with the rusted milk can of pegs.

You'd pin weighted, bleeding shirts all along the line
and I'd watch sea winds resurrect them into lightness.

NEW WINE IN AN OLD TEA URN

Each Sunday, many are called and columns
of cars crowd the car park, its puddles veined
with seeping diesel reflecting random
strains of weakened sunlight like broken stained

glass windows. They process to the breeze-blocked
community centre, dark Bibles kept
dry beneath rainbowed umbrellas, shadowed,
wired glass doors held wide open to accept

the gathered throng. Across the scuffed, varnished
floor of the rectangular sports hall,
chairs in circles surround the bespectacled
group in jeans and trainers, ready with guitars,

keyboard and tambourines to drown out those
slow silences of God. In wheelchairs shoved
out to the front, young men in ragged rows
wait expectantly for His longed for Word

to resound in their ears and make all clear.
Those who can, stand and sway and clap their hands
to the rousing music that vibrates air
in which disturbed dust beams dance in pale strands

of winter light. They mouth words projected
overhead, bending God's ear with deafening
praise: striving to erase dark times stretched
beneath striped duvets, headlights bewildering

their subdued wallpaper, hearing only
the distant echoes of their own prayers;
lying together and yet still lonely:
strangers beneath those protecting layers

of selves. They hold out their hands, palms upward,
as if to catch whatever crumbs He might
let fall, closing their minds to those awkward
questions that stalk through the stillness of night.

In the basketball court's centre circle,
the preacher, his direct lead to God trailing,
strikes apocalyptic notes through the crackle
of his microphone, professing joy unfailing.

At the end of the sermon – and the end
was a long time coming – the Saved join to talk
and line up for tea and angel cake then
take up their blue plastic chairs and walk.

PATTERNS OF CARPETS

Along labyrinthine corridors we walk,
door after door closing without a sound;
sunlight piercing glass like an open wound;
past rooms where only televisions talk.
Woven in patterns of carpets, guilt stalks
my steps, knowing that I'll leave you behind
and the long life we shared will reach it's end:
you unable to protest, struck dumb by a stroke.

I lead you to the room that will be home,
where almost all your needs will now be met –
except that inconvenient need for love.
From the lounge will come strains of Jim Reeves' songs.
Here, you'll knit dreams with yarns of light and wait
for night to caress you with once lost gloves.

FROM THE TRACTATUS TO TELETUBBYLAND

Only in moments does consciousness grow clear,
like a brief flame risen from moistened peat
and, with the self's emergence, comes the fear
of the return of that black winding sheet
that binds and smothers the once lucid mind
that penetrated the propositions
of the *Tractatus*. Like *Ivan* in his sack,
you struggle to break loose but cannot find
the opening to daylight's dimensions.
You reverse through darkness – driven far back

to bathe in those flowered fields, stems rigid,
beneath the bright sun's laughing, baby face
stuck in a high, arching sky of vivid,
bounded blue, before Copernicus.
There you roam through long days with pot-bellied
children who leap free of gravity's force
and fly kites that caress the firmament;
who live in a shadowless cave and eat jellied
custard that seeks out bowls; who sleep in peace,
safe where the mind's *death is not an event*

in life in that republic where unlived poems
are banned in those inarticulate
symposiums of summer when love's clean halves join
and the windmill on the hill rotates
through stillness, lightening air like fire
and rabbits graze beyond the reach of guns.
You shelter within those familiar stranger's hands
that cradle your unspeakable terror
as those round figures decline with the sun
into the silence that vibrates when music ends.

According to her husband, Iris Murdoch, in the grip of Alzheimer's disease, derived rare moments of comfort from watching 'Teletubbies'. She had been a great admirer of Plato and Wittgenstein. Words in italics from "Tractatus Logico-Philosophicus".

HEBRIDEAN HAIKU

Infancy

Adder coils of light;
bronchitic sea sucking rocks;
sun weeping gemstones.

Schooldays

Chalk dust particles
parachute on beeswaxed floors;
crows glare from stane dikes.

Youth

Letters knifed on birch
oozing bitter love juices;
corncrakes sawing dusk.

Parenthood

Pram wheels sunk in peat;
midges crowd wet alder leaves
silvered by summer.

Middle Age

Whooper swans like ghosts
on still lochs where rowans bleed
berries one by one ...

Old Age

Slow footfalls on shores
where tides leave gleaming jetsam
of long lost desires.

Death Bed

Waves flood spattered cliffs;
light somersaults over heads
of once loved strangers.

ONE JEWISH BOY

In the Realschule, you learned the facts of life,
collared, trussed and gazing out at the world
that *shows there is no such thing as the soul.*
Adolf stands erect at your back with folded
arms; starched, pristine shirt – winged as if for flight –
looking down on frozen columns of boys:
a held moment shuttered in black and white.

Two sets of searching, hypnotic eyes;
both with lips sealed, imprisoning those words
that would cast their spell to remove the spell
of self: the *Tractatus's* staccato;
the suffocations of that other's sentences:
the language that can illuminate or
kill. Safe in your garden shed, you awoke

to echoing notes of monastic bells
on summer dawns with traceries of dew
on islanded lawns when *the world and life
are one* while Adolf dreamed of bean rows of gallows
that choked the words from Jews:
cities cleansed of the chosen, their bodies
pendulous shadows in history's new dawn.

You turned your back on wealth as the *Godhead*
turned His back on platforms where suitcases
towered like Babels beneath His unshakeable silence.
The philosopher's fire casting intermittent beams
along the hung, labyrinthine galleries
of the mind strung with lamps like words
whose entrancing rays can reveal or blind.

In a recently discovered school photograph, Ludwig Wittgenstein appears to pose close to Adolf Hitler: they attended the same school at the same time. The title of the poem is taken from 'Mein Kampf'. Words in italics are taken from 'Tractatus Logico-Philosophicus'.

THE DESCENT

They find him hanging
from a rafter
in the barn:
his tongue blackened
and protruding
in contempt of life
but his toes
stretching towards
the log pile
as if he'd changed his mind:
too late.
Orange binder twine,
a little frayed,
grips his lengthened neck
as it grips the straw
head of a scarecrow
swollen on a rake
shaft, keeping wood pigeons
off the kale
in that unsteady,
early light
sea gives off.
His dungarees,
patched with cow dung,
bulge at the crotch
with its dried,
off-white stains
that would never
be removed.
His rigid body
sways in the breeze,
scented with neeps, the way it swayed
standing on the swing
as a child,

rising between elms,
their branches
taking the strain,
complaining
only a little
as the wet rope bruised
the seeping bark
in shafted sunlight
that penetrated
their translucent leaves.
Standing tall
and ascending,
head and shoulders
above them all,
gazing across
the Sound of Islay
at those fires
of heather
blackening slopes of Jura:
strands of smoke
lolling and thinning
as they rose
into spring air
when gorse
throws out
yellow petals
to light the moor.

His uncle, arms raised,
saws through the stranded
twine with a blunted
pruning knife,
then the father

takes hold
of his son
when he
descends to his
level.

TORCH

Pews burnished with beeswax
caught and held the sea's light,
strained through stained glass windows,
flooding the crucifix,
touched by dust motes in flight
from pressed worn ivories.

She moved the pedals:
music rose like water
from a well's darkened shaft,
bending back the candle's
searching tongue that fluttered
with the organ's long draught.

Slow waves echoed the hymns
that evening as they brushed
the rocks around the bay
and retreated in rings
on sand, sounding in hushed
voices, as if they prayed.

We stepped out of that church
with the dead around us
listening and waiting;
the sun's weakening torch
casting lighted pathways
of our own creating.

CAROUSEL OF SILENCES

A pair of worn hands at rest on a black tweed
skirt: that is all there is to see. Yet those deep
veined hands with their broken fingernails
reveal not only a life but a way of being.

Those hands that have spun and woven and dyed
the clothes you, your husband, your children
and grandchildren wore are now fixed forever
in a held moment of stillness. You have woven

yourself and your loved ones out of time. In the
unseen cottage, hewn out of rock and weighed down
with boulders in defiance of storms, I imagine
a dark, walled clock with its spindly arms

folded as one onto the soft lap of noon.
Beneath echoes of time, on the beeswaxed dresser,
that carousel of silences: a china dog guarding each corner;
blue patterned plates and bowls; green whisky bottles;

the framed icons of the Virgin: her face, moulded
into serenity, glazed by veils of sunlight stealing
through hair-fringed window eyes. Outside, those uneven
pyramids of peat still glistening wet from deep layers

of moor where I see your bowed, shawled head shrouded
by midges. I catch that burnt honey scent of gorse
and picture black cattle daydreaming in mauves
of heather, ghosted by moist breaths of sea winds.

I see you also, bent double beneath a wicker
creel of seaweed, salt water streaming down your
back like smelting silver in afternoons of spring
with peewits preening and strutting between lazybeds.

A lifetime of joy and suffering scoured on hands
which you display with deep acceptance and pride as
if you sensed that you and your kind were the last
of a royal line with that crown of scythed, gold-flecked

oats in encircled stooks, angling across stoned fields in the
taken breath of a September evening, waulked by fingers of
moonlight, with green and silver bands of mackerel winding
beneath the translucent surface of the gouged eye of bay.

Those photographed hands live on like lived poems
while you, forever faceless, lie in the island's sparse soil.
The life of you and your kind like stories knitted
around a stubborn fire to keep the warmth within.

In 1954 the great American photographer, Paul Strand spent three
months in South Uist, and recorded a traditional way of life that was
soon to change. One of Strand's most haunting images consists simply
of a pair of aged hands resting on the knees of a faceless woman.

GLOBED LAMP

You trimmed the lamp when the lights went out,
your face drowning in paraffin fumes
that rose to cloud spaces on the ceiling,
mapped with where the distemper was.

You could never disperse those circles of smoke
that ascended with the shadows' climb
as you searched for the pure, blue flame
that would illumine the mounted photograph

of you in your pressed khaki uniform:
a soldier before the bullets came.
A gust would shift the unswept soot
from the flue; logs would spit as they turned

to redden their undersides to ash
as you later turned on the hospital bed
as if to view the high shielded light
from differing angles of perception:

clearing the drugged rings from your eyes;
opening the hinged, glass door of the world
to tamper with the living wick
in your search for that true, tongued flame.

TONGUES OF FLAME
(In Memory Of Alasdair Maclean)

How will they know they are beautiful if I do not tell them so?

Those shy hill lochans of Ardnamurchan
you told were beautiful are beautiful still
but you are no longer there to tell them.

They lie alone in hollows with cupped
hands, brimful of moonlight that cuts
silver swathes across the Atlantic ocean.

The stoned fields in which your father gouged
a living are now bereft of sheep; *Kerr's Pink*
no longer flower each summer, their white blossom

drifting like snow. The hen-house door flaps and
flaps all day, unable to close the past which
insists on being heard; left feathers parachute from

perches to layer the floor deep with droppings
which your mother will never again sweep clean,
her floured apron crossed around her chest.

The few, named cattle stand no more up
to their knees in the lush grass of spring,
their sleek coats altering with shadow and with light.

On the moor where bog cotton dances
in breezes, the open wound of your peat
bank has not quite healed, its wet face

gleams on. A broken cairn of unlifted peat
waits patiently to be taken home but that fire
around which you sat, a returning stranger,

has long since gone out: dowsed by death.
But the poems you wrote out of love
and pain and anger smoulder on, ready

to ignite into tongues of flame like those
sudden slithers of sunlight that broke from
dreich skies, glancing off the honed blade

of your father's relentless, rhythmic scythe.

LATE NIGHT PHONE-IN

I'm on my own now and I sit here,
headphoned behind glass, listening to voices
of strangers who talk to me as if to their
most intimate friend, or, perhaps, their only
friend. I listen. I talk. I listen.
I swivel to look down on lights
syringing the black water of the river
that veins this city where, it seems, only

the exhausted or the contented can sleep,
wrapped in warm duvets: stepping out
into the strange, silenced land of dreams.
These remain awake, drawing comfort from voices
of damaged others they carry into kitchens,
living-rooms, bedrooms to drown out faint echoes
of absence that stalks through midnight flats where
some solitary listener has dined at a table set for two.

He left a note of explanation that didn't
explain nothing ... We was alright at the start
until he began to use me as his punch-bag ...
It's like I've lost my right arm ... know what I mean?
You know, mother doesn't recognize me no more ...
it's like living with a stranger:
the bewildered, inarticulate callers merge but
the aching uniqueness of each cliché remains.

I put on another CD to punctuate
those ungrammatical expressions of despair
and while *All By Myself* whines on, I look
around this single-seated confessional and wonder
how much longer I can continue this weekly
rite when I have no penances to give, no
absolution to offer, only my voice sounding out
into the urban wilderness of each Saturday night.

THE DESTINED JOURNEY OF ETTY HILLESUM

*I am with the hungry, with the ill-treated and the dying, every day, but I
am also with the jasmine and with that piece of sky beyond my window;
there is room for everything in a single life.*

I often think of you, Etty, gazing longingly
at that light gathering tree which stands
outside your bedroom window like a cross.

That tree mirrors your moods as a stilled
lake mirrors the sky where clouds darken,
then disperse, pierced by swords of sunlight.

I watch you at your loved desk with its uneven
pyramid of books: Rilke, Dostoevsky, St. Augustine ...
your head bowed, wielding your pen like a hammer

to beat pathways through layers of your bewildering
selves; recording the mysterious ways of your lovers;
those almost suicidal periods of despair; the sudden,

unlooked for revelations of beauty and inexpressible joy
and that overpowering need to simply kneel and murmur
soft words to One you could not begin to comprehend.

In my dreams, you walk through the mud of
Westerbork still, in rags, turning your gaze beyond
the barbed wire to where fields of yellow lupins dance

in sun kissed waves of July winds, their peppered
scent pervading your lungs as you pause to sit on a
rock and write love letters to the life you've left behind.

In the deepest recesses of night, I glimpse
the broken beams of your torch as you help mothers
lift their children, rigid with terror, onto cattle trucks

on their long journey along tracks, with no dividing
lines, to where chimneys tower: tracks you knew you
soon must follow. Afterwards, when sleep is slow to blind,

you watch loving fingers of moonlight cradle the transit
camp with willow wands of smelted silver; across untroubled
skies, stars create decipherable patterns of diamonds.

When you finally board your destined wagon, number 12,
you move outwith my vision but I hear the frail song
you sang echo ever louder through the years and I sense

you sing on somewhere in a land beyond all my
imaginings where you walk, hand in hand, with all those
lost children through unfenced fields of golden lupins.

FOLDS

The subsidence of mounds of leaves
that fold over in layers as they burn
when dusk shortens the drive to the castle
lighting oblongs on the river that folds
lines of smudged silver over the weir.

Apples folded in yesterday's news;
waxed skin printed with the lives of others:
all those traumas transmuted into scent
to fill the attic, its rafters articulating rain
which folds with flecks down drains.

Those pressed folds of sheets on hospital beds
starched by sunlight through wide windows
where emptied cars wait out afternoons in squares,
bordered by marigolds, liveried by dust
that falls in folds over spaced kerbstones.

The folds of soil as it descends on graves
when the green canvas, drawn in with strings of frost,
is folded back to reveal the opening below us;
our feet loosening the knots of sawn boards
diagramed with the folds of their grain.

Those folds of light when mist lifts up from lochs
like vinegared windows rained with sea;
the folds of water pushed aside by oars
with descended swans' wings drawn
back and folded in their resting place.

AFTER DARK

He takes you out for an airing after dark
when rain has slackened its hold of the river,
past the chained swings that hang limp in the park
where the reflections of plane trees shiver
across the heightened pond. Joined by the hand,
you move together past the lighted lives
of others, climbing the brae, leaving the town:
its talking behind backs, words scarring like knives;
the stares of strangers; night streets that lamps strand;
stepping on narrow, strawed farm roads that drown

the echoes of motion. Night after night,
you follow in the footsteps of father's shame,
revealed by a late car's unforgiving light,
he turns his head, unable to confront the blame.
You struggle to speak but no words can be traced:
language defeats you so you hit out in anger,
your free hand flailing at nothing in the dark.
You disturb puddles where diesel strands linger,
then some drowning, distorted stranger's face
looms up at you, mocking your cries when dogs bark

from the still lit, uncurtained, bay window
that glares down on the lawn where elm branches
move shadows in the night sky's mysterious glow
before morning lights the wings of chaffinches
showering themselves in shallow pools that streams
recycle. You pass the churchyard by the bridge
where the dead are kept behind bars in rows
for ease of counting. Birches form a ridge
along the river whose sounds flow into your dreams
and you begin to falter as its motion slows

until sudden, scented winds brush back your hair
and an owl measures night's depths with its call
in those remembered moments you can share
when your hands weld and your separate steps fall
as one on moss that joins fractured pavements:
remaining awake while unknowing others sleep,
listening to sounds only night can bring,
running fingers across daylight's undersides;
held and kept afloat beyond words' currents
where silence and darkness merge in waves to sing.

A Free Church elder would only take his brain damaged son out under cover of darkness as he felt he had been punished by God.

TERMINUS

As he steps onto the bus, he feels the belt tighten around
his waist. He pays his fare – avoiding the driver's eyes.

He walks slowly up the aisle, trying not to look at those
smiling children's faces. He stands, gripping the rail, counting

the passengers adding up in front of him. He thinks
of the button. He prays. He thinks of the button. He prays.

He pictures the paradise that awaits him
like those blank outlines he coloured in as a child:

the shining face of Allah and the seventy-two
Virgins with their open, alabaster arms.

He'll feel nothing, they told him, as they gave him his testament
– they wrote: he intoned the words like a true believer.

They placed the Koran in his hands and the camera
flashed again and again: fixing his fate on stills,

before he played the destined role of himself on video.
The bits, that were him, will litter those Israeli streets

but he shall be whole in that land where streams flow
free of blood. Not one of them, in front of him, is innocent –

no, don't look at the children's faces: he remembers the way
his father looked with the astonishment of death in his eyes:

that black hole where his chest should be; mother's arms frozen
around Ibrahim; screams of jets shredding his Palestinian sky.

He lifts his eyes to the backs of those Jewish heads –
he looks only to the front. Thank God he can no longer

see the faces. His hand reaches for the button
without him ...

SPELLS

*When we have passed a certain age, the soul of the child that we were and
the souls of the dead from whom we sprang, come and shower upon us
their riches and their spells.*
– Marcel Proust.

I hold within myself everyone who has gone before,
they pile up like those beech leaves I burned as a child;
the neat heaps raked along the drive above Port Askaig,
the rows of fires reddening at dusk, the shiver of the sea
at high tide when dark waves threatened to overflow the pier.
The loose sheets of newspaper blown by sudden gusts
opening and closing like a secret volume of my past;
the sulphur of the match igniting into flames of remembrance.
In the darkness, those fires shone like stars and the lighthouse
on the skerry revolved its spaced lights like answering prayers.

Sometimes my dead father gazes out at me from oval mirrors,
I see soap suds ooze down his face with a shock of recognition.
I hear the scrape, scrape of his blunted Wilkinson Sword.
His eyes are less accusing than once they were, less disappointed
as though he stood looking down from some plateau of forgiveness.
We merge into each other and out again like those wavering
reflections we left on the surface of Loch Allen when we
dipped our varnished oars into peated water, raised them
to let fall globes of water like separate worlds, made translucent
by sudden shafts of sunlight which brushed monogamous swans.

I could never really talk to you, mother, when you were alive,
smoke signals might have been more effective than words.
I see you still standing behind the plate glass of that hospital
window,wrapped in your loosening blue dressing gown,
waving what was to be your last goodbye. How long did you go
on waving after my car had drifted out of the car park to join
the lighted flow? I recall you waving your flowered dish towel as

the ferry left the pier and passed below our white house perched
on the wooded cliff, your frantic towel shaking out rooks from beech
trees as I was moved towards the mainland of my childish dreams.

And you, darling, I seem to just miss you everywhere I go:
I step into rooms you have only recently exited, I catch
the perfume you've left behind. I crawl between sheets imprinted
with your body, I stretch into the oblivion of sleep listening
to the rhythm of your lost breaths. I cannot break free of the now
insubstantial figures my pasts, they cling to me like those cotton
winged seeds of fireweed which colonize sites of dereliction with blaze
after blaze of waving magenta which dances in wind and sunlight.
I move towards my future grasping the vein-less hands
of ghosts, not knowing if I lead or if I follow.

THE LIVES AND DEATHS OF ST.KILDA

It was in the scented breath of the west
wind that the *Sluagh* came: death crossing sea
in formation, shadowing each wave's crest,
veering towards us on the sun touched lee
of our island awash with ominous
signs. Mystery weighs us down like those stone
weights that hang from our heathered, roped-down roofs;
our high, spattered cliffs cannot defend us;
we listen to that wind's invading drone
and with each laboured breath, we inhale death's.

On those motionless evenings when sunlight
dissolves into shadows on fulmars' wings,
coffins float across bouldered fields on slight
poles', corn crushed by grave, guided feet, frail rings
of fire from dying embers of soaked peat
smouldering, flickering in fulmar oil
encased in lamps of stone: unearthly lights
pushing the darkness back. The winding sheet
of sea barely breathes below us as we toil
to where the dead command the chilled heights.

Unprotesting children bedded beneath
turf at evening: half-grown coffins ensconced
in peat; stilled bells of heather forming wreaths
of dark purple unmoving in response
to the death of wind: a coarsened blanket
that only those returning gales will fold:
one black dwelling exchanged for another.
We breathe the peat smoke then the peated
moor breathes us in great, moist lungfuls of cold
air like some possessed, consuming lover.

Our dead are more restless than the living,
they shift to inhabit stones, cliffs, birds, burns,
unable to gain the stillness they're longing
for: even on those hushed afternoons when surf turns
slowly and cormorants hang out their wings
to dry on smoothed, slimed rocks stuck with limpets;
time's torn shadow encircles the sundial
of stones; across the Sound, a stretched seal sings
and the smoked lamp flame of the sun's brief light
strands the clouds: the dead's relentless trial

does not cease. We pray for deliverance
but the dead are delivered back to us
in shapes we cannot decipher; they dance
in those slivers of light that sea loses
and that rocks reflect when struck by the moon's
ghosted beams. On this island, the living
and the dead merge unseeing into each
other: separation is useless. Flames
from turf rise each night up our walls, stretching
like tired children but too shadowy to touch.

Before the coming of Christianity to St.Kilda, dead children were always laid to rest at evening. The Sluagh was a terrifying portent of approaching death.

A LIFT

Blue blisters of paint
burst on the unhinged door
as she makes her headlong
journey to the grave;
rising and falling
as if on a remembered
roller-coaster ride
down the narrow, winding stairs
no coffin could ascend:
her eyelids pressed tight
as if she daren't look;
her hair falling loose
at last; her white frilled nightgown
still tucked demurely around
her trim, wasted ankles:
eaten alive
but not by midges.

In the scullery,
the lidless coffin waits
to give her a lift,
its brass handles shimmering
in a sluggish stream
of late autumn sunlight
riddled through the net curtains
which cave into the breeze
that finds its way beneath
the barely raised, corded window.

Outside, hens leave
their splayed footprints
across the whitened lawn
and the skeletoned fingers
of the last horse chestnut leaves
lift to reveal their jaundiced underbellies
in the pale gleams of light
which the sea returns.

In the front porch,
coal lumps in a tea-chest
glisten with melted frost.

FINDING THE DARKNESS
(Sestina For Wittgenstein In Connemara)

I can only think clearly in the dark and in Connemara I have
found one of the last pools of darkness in Europe.

I see you standing alone in darkness
in that garden hedged with wet fuchsias,
listening intently to the strange language
of seabirds who ghost above Atlantic waves;
broken sentences of staccato lights
from the skerry interrupting your thoughts.

Often, specters of death would stalk your thoughts
like fluttering storm petrels in darkness,
their deep set eyes pinpricked with lights.
Breezes would shake stamens of fuchsias,
pebbled shores would be shoved aside by waves
of the vast sea's bewildering language.

In the Tractatus, you opened language
to make a window for the world of thoughts
but the Irish tongue surged in spuming waves,
dancing in reels of their verbal darkness
as pearls of rain balanced on fuchsias
and the sky was ribboned with shafts of lights.

From the eyes of cottages, all the lights
have gone; you imagine the lost language
of famished men who lay beneath fuchsias
in storms, dead children ghosting through their thoughts.
Where is God, to whom you prayed, in darkness?
You listen to silences between waves.

Each day, you watch gannets explode in waves;
cormorants hang their wings in shifting lights
when watered sun folds back sheets of darkness
from this land which is woven in language:
each field, pool, rock are named, where words and thoughts
are layered like turf, brushed by fuchsias.

The stilled air is heavy with fuchsias'
honeyed scent, midges rise as one in waves
from soaked moss; clarity enters your thoughts
like sudden arrow showers tipped with lights;
luminous as scoured landscape and language
in sudden revelations of darkness.

Above high fuchsias, you glimpse strange lights
that drown in waves, unsayable language
beyond thoughts: you reach to embrace darkness.

THE BISCUIT BARREL

It was the only prize you ever won,
that biscuit barrel with the silvered rim,
untouched and untainted by any crumb.
It smugly watched its squat reflection swim
in the sea's light that flooded the dresser,
polished on fuchsia-blown afternoons
of summer, no mounted clock could measure;
with drifting scents of warming, rising scones
from that Aga with a mind of its own.
It sat there, waiting, like an empty urn,
mirroring moving shadows of flames thrown
by the brass fender when scorched beech logs turned
and fell when you died in the room above
that barrel shaped and altered by your love.

ISLAND INCIDENT

He passes the restless hens
with their feathers erect,
showering themselves in dust pools
that autumn sunbeams reflect.

They shelter beneath fuchsias
whose stamens reach out beyond
their red, drooping petals
that surround the motionless pond.

He comes in sight of the house:
whitewash darkening on its walls
beneath the tall sycamore trees
where a lengthening shadow falls.

Flecks of paint pattern his shoes
when he knocks on the blistered door;
he stares anxiously around
as footsteps echo across the floor.

Cautiously, the door grinds open,
unused to being disturbed,
she gazes out into the sunlight:
her searching eyes still blurred.

I've come for eggs, he mutters.
She recognizes him: the lank hair,
gaunt face, those restless hands,
the eyes staring into mid-air.

Reluctantly, she invites him in,
sunlight smudged against frosted glass;
pale petals fall from pelargoniums
as she steps aside to let him pass.

He goes into the living-room
where brief shadows of faltering flames
from reddening peat behind bars
cross the yellow ceiling like veins.

Folds of faded chrysanthemums smother
the settee and the massive armchair;
above the fire, a gamekeeper looks down:
shotgun ready, Labradors scenting the air.

I'll just get the eggs from the larder:
her rarely used voice uncertain in tone;
sunlight penetrates the meshed window
and spreads itself in pieces across stone.

Carefully, she positions each brown egg,
stuck with pale straw strands
into the hollows of white polystyrene
which faintly squeals in her hands.

He follows each movement she makes
as he leans forward from the chair,
he watches her skirt gently sway,
her flushed face brushed by her hair.

Across the singed rug, he steps
silently in his polished shoes
on which strange reflections shimmer:
beyond hope, with no more to lose.

She turns and holds out the eggs
as if in offering, her mouth open,
but he doesn't hear her scream:
at her feet, egg shells lie broken.

He hears the polystyrene squeal louder
and louder, a trapped bee drones;
he sees orange yolks, streaked with red,
leak down and pattern the flagstones.

FRAGMENTS OF EDEN

*The wrinkles and creases on our faces are the registration of the great
passions, vices, insights that called on us; but we, the masters, were not
at home.*
– Walter Benjamin.

In the photograph in front of me, your head is bowed
as if with the weight of the world; your chin
rests of your smooth, delicate hand; your eyes,
behind thick spectacles, hold deep oceans of sadness.

And yet, in middle-age, you have the look of a mysteriously
engrossed child. No one was was more at home
to experiences than you. As with Kafka and Proust, the age
left its deepest mark on one furthest removed from it.

Like a honey bee hovering over dewed fields of clover,
you gathered the pollen traces of this world and sifted
them through fine mesh in search of precious fragments
of truth left behind like blown rose petals from Eden.

As a child collects shells to listen to altering tones
of sea, your study was towered not just with books but
newspapers, advertisements, postage stamps, albums, circulars:
in everything you deciphered the broken spirit of the age.

You retained in your capacious memory, remarks
overheard in the Paris streets along which you loved to
stroll: the flaneur in whom nothing was ever lost.
You filled volumes with quotations which would reveal

truths if placed in a defining order, with no commentary
from you, the invisible author, paring his fingernails.
You distilled like nectar from lilacs, the wisdom from
stories and sudden, dazzling revelations from poems.

As a translator, you searched for that pristine language
that lies like long buried jewels beneath the cacophony
of conflicting tongues. For you, as for St. John, in the beginning
was the Word and the Word is, ultimately, all there is.

I picture your body slumped in that bare hotel room
in Port Bou after you dreamed your way to death
through morphine induced images of your past like a
drowning man encountering images of his former selves.

How sad that there was no one there to witness in your
last expressions that unforgettable beauty and authority
which the storyteller borrows from the dying and which even
the poorest wretch possesses for the living around him.

Still, you whose every thought was itself a poem, live on
in the arcades of memory as I walk these Paris boulevards
past headlines and billboards and neon lights as dusk descends,
observing all those disjointed signs only you could make whole.

LAUNDERED TOWELS

A man of business who could sign his name
no longer, you practiced behind closed doors,
forming each letter, concealing your shame,
rewriting your identity with more
scrawled pages each day: words blinded by pain.

Drowning, you grappled with that buoyancy
only names can give, floating on oceans
beyond sight of land beneath vacancies
of sky, drifting on rising waves' motions;
captured in bewildering currencies

outwith your control. I found your notebooks
hidden in drawers of laundered towels,
days after you died; currents of air shook
the loose pages as I held them, gusts filed
beneath the lifted, corded window; rooks

let winds carry their caws through rifled woods;
strangled branches balancing careless nests.
I saw your listed name dissolve in floods
of ink like half-forgotten writing tests:
copperplate with damaged nibs in childhood

through long afternoons of thin, gold stars
for others; those effortless sounds of sea.
I read the intended *f* with no bar;
I followed the broken cross of each *t*;
the space, then the recline, of that last *r*.

At the onset of Alzheimer's disease, a middle-aged business man
gradually forgot how to form the letters of his own name, so he
practised his signature in secret.

TEA DANCE ON A TUESDAY AFTERNOON

Across the floor, the ageing couples glide,
chintz curtains drawn against the afternoon,
along streamer walls, their silhouettes slide
in slow foxtrots in a makeshift ballroom.
They dance and dream as one, lined cheek to cheek,
as fraying tape unwinds from spool to spool:
lifting brief moments out of time each week,
in measuring time to music's schedule.
Around their thickening waists, women feel
men's arms – lost in that ache of cheap perfume;
dimmed stationary lights begin to reel
in ghosts of waltzes that ended too soon.
Against the day's harsh light, they weave romance:
knowing it's not too late to dance, dance, dance ...

LANGUAGES OF BABYLE
(At the Grave of Iain Crichton Smith)

It is always in autumn that I see you,
walking hand in hand with Donalda
along the esplanade in Oban, past the cathedral
with its organ notes made discordant by sea winds.

Across the bay, the spaced lights of Kerrera
burn more brightly with the deepening dusk;
as you slowly walk, you listen to the gulls'
strangely human cries of exile and longing.

Images of autumn flooded your mind like
the high tides of Babyle where your languages
were confused by humans and not by God:
that unbending figure in whom you could never believe.

Here where your mother's footsteps crushed the frail
daffodils each spring when she followed the narrow path
to the moor, with a creel strapped to her back, where cairns
of peat were shot through with scattered pellets of sunlight.

Those leaping salmon psalms she sung in the Free Kirk
each Sunday resounded in your ears long after
her shrill voice had gone and, despite your loathing,
were echoed in the sonorous cadences of your verse.

Not far from your home in Taynuilt, the granite statue
of Duncan Ban MacIntyre stands still, gazing stalker-like
down across Loch Awe where *the deer move out
in isolated air* and wet rowans shake their bowed

heads in a breeze, letting fall their berries like droplets
of claret on goose-fleshed water. Those threatening,
scheming voices that whispered in your tortured mind
have all been lulled to silence now and cattle cough

ghostlike through the mists of autumn beyond
the cemetery walls of Muckairn where you lie with one
ear strained to hear the wailing choirs of the distant ocean
that will forever call you home to wind-bent grasses.

Here now is the *stubborn place* of which you wrote
where the bewildering metaphors by which you
lived no longer swarm like midges around this blunt fact
but, as a fellow traveller through verbal mazes wrote:

the facts of this world are not the end of the matter.

*Iain Crichton Smith grew up in the crofting township of Babyle in the Isle
of Lewis. Although Gaelic was his native language, he was taught entirely
in English and he felt divided between two languages all his life.
The poem's final line is a quotation from Ludwig Wittgenstein.*

THE RESURRECTION OF GILBERT KAPLAN

As those closing bars gave way to a reverberating
silence, something long frozen within you thawed
like the ice floes of an Alpine river in spring sunlight.

You sensed that nothing would ever be the same
again after hearing that choir's voices soar as if to
assault the heavens and those last trumpets call from afar.

In everyone's life, perhaps, there are moments which
hold within themselves the promise of renewal but we
lack the courage to follow them wherever they might lead.

Moments like certain angles of light on a hill lochan
at evening when the sun gives up the ghost behind
stoned hills and sheep bleat to the rhythm of waves

slowly advancing and retreating, advancing and
retreating on bouldered shores; a moored lobster
boat rising and falling, rising and falling ...

the stilled air weighted with salt and peat smoke evoking
memories one can't quite hold on to like the dark
water of a rushing burn which leaves faint traces

of itself on our chilled fingers. You, Gilbert, travelled
the earth in pursuit of one who *surrendered* himself
to the music which was *dictated* to him like a man

who follows the urgent promptings of love and fate.
Your fixed your eyes on the motions of maestros;
you immersed yourself in that miraculous score

like a deep sea diver exploring the beds of oceans.
You became the symphony you dreamed of conducting
until, one day, your dream was fulfilled and music

flowed from your guided fingertips, your slim baton
conjouring decipherable patterns through air.
The symphony must be a world, said Mahler

and you recreated this glorious world with your own
rhythmic hands, carving unimaginable sounds
like a sculptor who frees the form within the stone.

Like you, we unknowingly long for something other:
for some rebirth of what we once possessed, our
voices, at last, answering that persistent echo within.

The life of the Wall Street financier, Gilbert Kaplan was transformed by hearing Mahler's Resurrection Symphony. Despite his limited musical knowledge, he eventually achieved his dream by conducting and recording this symphony.

ABSENCE

I read about your death in the local newspaper.
There was no grained photograph of you: you were
faceless to the end. In death, you took your
place among reports of road accidents; drunken brawls;
bingo wins; notices of planning consent; lottery
numbers; the latest football results – lower league.

Like me, you came from the Highlands to live in this
Lowland town but you were a stranger to me – you were
a stranger to everyone. I may have passed you many times on
the street; perhaps I brushed against you in the crowded aisle
of the supermarket: our shoulders may have touched, if only for
an instant: an unregistered meeting of separate loneliness.

The coroner *could not ascertain* how you died:
a precise verdict defeated by days, weeks, months of decay.
A soiled till receipt, dated 15 November, was found lying
like a fallen birch leaf beneath the Formica topped table
revealing the recorded details of your final purchase: three cans
of *Del Monte* peaches – on *Special Offer* in *Spar* that day.

I imagine bills and circulars flowing through your
letter-box each week to form an unstable cairn on the hall mat:
mail sorted by official fingers seeking for the address
of a friend or relative. Mould would form and creep across
unwashed dishes. The cold water tap in the sink might drip and
drip like a metronome measuring the beat of unheard music.

Time would go on passing even after the battery in
your wall clock died: its spindly arms shuddering to a halt.
The pages of your calendar remained unturned after November:
perhaps depicting, like mine, sunlit Highland cattle up to their
knees in a burn; those curlicues of smoke from a croft house
chimney stretching and thinning into a lucid, interminable sky.

I read that on the mantelpiece above your electric, barred
fire, the wedding portrait of your dead parents gazed out
helplessly from an oval frame, signed *Lochinver Free Church, 1949*,
as you lay silenced and slumped on that bed, guarding your
secrets to the end in that flat whose rented rooms resounded
with your absence more palpably than they did with your presence.

Some nights when sleep evades me like a dissolved dream,
I hear owls calling with the ghosted voices of lost strangers
hovering and swooping above the lives they might have lived.

EINSTEIN IN CROMER

Lamplight casts shadows on wooden walls;
musical notes counterpoint the raindrops
which drum and drum on the corrugated roof.

Below you, the night waves of the North Sea
endlessly fold back the pebbles on the shore,
and gulls cry out for something they have lost.

Reality moves further and further away from you
like the tail lights of a train through a tunnel,
moving faster and faster beyond the speed of light.

Everything around you seems shifting and insubstantial:
your body, your mind, time, matter, your beliefs,
the faces of those who walk the streets of your childhood.

The news from home is not good: hunger, humiliation,
torture, murder and the hounding to suicide of one you love
while you, self-absorbed as always, follow the bewildering

labyrinths of the atom like those dusty corridors in attics
which Kafka's ghostly figures followed where the accused
stand endlessly with bowed head awaiting the sentence

for some nameless crime: a verdict from which there
is no reprieve. *God does not play dice with the universe,*
you once said but the dice you rolled into the heart of matter

displayed life and death on all six sides.

*In 1933, Einstein was forced to flee Nazi Germany and on the way to the
USA, he spent a number of weeks in a hut outside Cromer in Norfolk. His
scientific discoveries at this time led to the creation of the atomic bomb.*